Written by **Karen Krossing** | Illustrated by **Dawn Lo**

One

Tiny

Bubble

The Story of Our
Last Universal
Common Ancestor

Owlkids Books

Long, long ago,

before you took your first breath,
before your parents were born and your grandparents
    and great-grandparents, too,
even before any dinosaurs hatched or algae began to
    grow in the seas,

lived your first family member,

LUCA*

*LUCA stands for Last Universal Common Ancestor.
Your family tree begins with LUCA.

Imagine Earth way back then,
when meteorites crashed from outer space,
lightning storms flashed,
volcanoes erupted,
and waves churned over rocks.
Within this unfriendly world, LUCA came to life.

LUCA was a squishy blob with no legs or arms.
No eyes or mouth.
Tinier than a cupcake sprinkle,
   it triggered mighty changes on our planet.

LUCA formed from
the dust of exploded stars,

water that made it a muddy soup,

and a lot of heat.

Scientists think LUCA came to life
at the bottom of a sea
in bubbling water
warmed by the red-hot core of the Earth.

Wherever it happened, the muddy ingredients boiled.

Then one tiny bubble ballooned into a thin membrane around some of the mixture,

around ingredients just right to create the first member of your family—

to create LUCA.

LUCA was just one cell
   held together by its membrane,
      while you are many cells
         held together by your skin.
It absorbed food,
      although it didn't have a stomach.

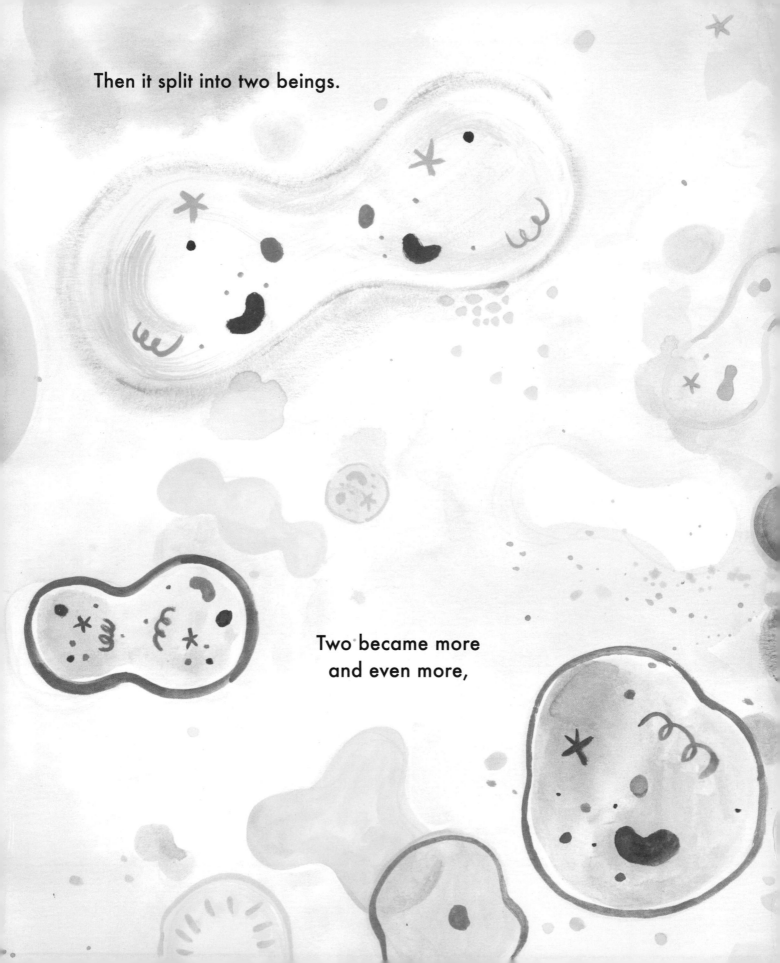

Then it split into two beings.

Two became more
and even more,

each growing
and some changing.

Over billions of years, these
descendants of LUCA evolved into
ancient algae
and giant dinosaurs . . .

... mushrooms and moss,
fir trees and ferns,
bacteria and bedbugs,

sea stars and sharks,
lizards and lions . . .

. . . your great-grandparents, your grandparents,
your parents, and now . . . you.

You belong to the oldest family on Earth.

Your LUCA family connects you to all life on the planet—
far and near,
old and young,
too big to hold,
and too small to see
with just your eyes.

You are one of Earth's miracles
that began with one tiny bubble
in just the right place,
made of just the right ingredients—

a miracle that could be repeated
on another world among the stars.

About LUCA

LUCA stands for our Last Universal Common Ancestor. LUCA was not the first life-form to exist on Earth, but it was the **last** one before life began to branch into many different and unique beings. **Universal** means it affects all beings within a group. Over billions of years, all living beings developed from the same ingredients that made LUCA, and every life-form now on Earth shares this one **common** ancestor. An **ancestor** is any life that came before you in your family, such as a grandparent or great-grandparent.

Scientists discovered LUCA by tracing our shared tree of life through our genes. A gene is a basic unit of information that determines the traits you inherit from your parents, such as your height. Every living thing on the planet belongs to one family tree, starting with LUCA.

We can only guess at how LUCA first formed because no one was around to witness it over three billion years ago. Exactly where on Earth did LUCA first appear? How did the first membrane and cell develop? What forms of life existed before LUCA, and why did they die out? We may never know for sure.

Scientists also wonder if life may have formed on other planets or moons in the same way it did here. Although our nearby planets and moons seem like hostile places for new life, ancient Earth was also hostile. What if another tiny bubble had once formed on a faraway planet in just the right place and made of just the right ingredients? What if you could meet the family who descended from that bubble—one as miraculous as our LUCA family?

Words to Know

To **absorb** means to take in or soak up.

A **cell** is the smallest building block of a living thing.

A **descendant** is a life-form that is related in a direct line to those who lived at an earlier time. You are a descendant of your parents, grandparents, and so on.

To **evolve** means to slowly grow and change over a long period of time. All of Earth's living creatures evolved from LUCA.

A **membrane** is a thin, flexible layer around a cell.

A **meteorite** is a large hunk of rock that crashes into a planet's surface.

Sources

Cooper, Keith. "Looking for LUCA, the Last Universal Common Ancestor." *NASA Astrobiology*, March 30, 2017. Online.

Wade, Nicholas. "Meet Luca, the Ancestor of All Living Things." *The New York Times*, July 25, 2016. Online.

Weiss, Madeline C., Filipa L. Sousa, Natalia Mrnjavac, Sinje Neukirchen, Mayo Roettger, Shijulal Nelson-Sathi, and William F. Martin. "The physiology and habitat of the last universal common ancestor." *Nature Microbiology*, Article number 16116, July 25, 2016. Online.

To our LUCA family—K.K.

To all the new beginnings that are yet to come—D.L.

The author would like to thank Dr. William F. Martin of the Institute of Molecular Evolution at Heinrich-Heine-Universität Düsseldorf for generously sharing his time and expertise to review the text. Any errors are solely the author's.

Owlkids Books acknowledges the financial support of the Canada Council for the Arts, the Ontario Arts Council, the Government of Canada through the Canada Book Fund (CBF) and the Government of Ontario through the Ontario Creates Book Initiative for our publishing activities.

Published in Canada by Owlkids Books Inc., 1 Eglinton Avenue East, Toronto, ON M4P 3A1
Published in the US by Owlkids Books Inc., 1700 Fourth Street, Berkeley, CA 94710

Library of Congress Control Number: 2021951169

Library and Archives Canada Cataloguing in Publication

Title: One tiny bubble / written by Karen Krossing ; illustrated by Dawn Lo.
Names: Krossing, Karen, author. | Lo, Dawn, 1992- illustrator.
Identifiers: Canadiana 20210376457 | ISBN 9781771474450 (hardcover)
Subjects: LCSH: Life—Origin—Juvenile literature. | LCSH: Evolution (Biology)—Juvenile literature.
Classification: LCC QH325 .K76 2022 | DDC j576.8/3—dc23

Edited by Stacey Roderick | Designed by Alisa Baldwin

Manufactured in Shenzhen, Guangdong, China, in March 2022, by WKT Co. Ltd.
Job #21CB3385

A   B   C   D   E   F

Publisher of Chirp, Chickadee and OWL
www.owlkidsbooks.com | Owlkids Books is a division of bayard canada